AF616817

"There is an old proverb that says 'Thoughts disentangle themselves when passing over the lips and through the finger tips.' The 17:18 Series, which encourages us to actually write out the words of Scripture, will be a tremendous tool in putting that proverb into action in our daily lives. I am happy to commend this project."

–Jerry Bridges, a longtime staff member of the Navigators and author of *The Pursuit of Holiness*

"Several years ago I read an article about copying the Scriptures by hand. I tried it with the Pastoral Epistles, writing out all three books with a fountain pen in my journal, and found it a profitable exercise. I am glad to see this series of journals appear, and I hope they are widely used."

–Donald S. Whitney, Associate Professor of Biblical Spirituality, The Southern Baptist Theological Seminary, Louisville

The 17:18 Series

The Book of Leviticus

Joel R. Beeke and Rob Wynalda

This book belongs to:

____

Given by: _______________________

Date: __________________________

Leviticus

Published by
Reformation Heritage Books
2965 Leonard St. NE
Grand Rapids, MI 49525
616-977-0889 / Fax 616-285-3246
e-mail: orders@heritagebooks.org
website: www.heritagebooks.org

ISBN 978-1-60178-656-2

Cover Design: Bethany Sanderson and Steve Coy
Journible® Design: Rob Wynalda

Jhy the 17:18 series?

ı Deuteronomy 17, Moses is leaving final instructions
oncerning the future of Israel. As a prophet of God,
noses foretells of when Israel will place a king over the
ation (v. 14). In verses 16 & 17, he lists items that the
ing could not do as king. In verse 18, he transitions to
hat he should do as king.

he king is commanded not to simply acquire a copy of
he law (the entire book of Deuteronomy) from the "scroll
ublishing house," but to handwrite his own copy of the law.
he purpose of such a copy written by his own hand was
o that:

* he would read it
* he would learn to fear the Lord
* he would obey the commands of God
* his heart would not become proud
* he would not turn to the right or the left from following the law (Prov. 4:27)
* also, his sons would serve in the kingdom after him (Deut. 17:19, 20).

hirty-four hundred years later, educators are
iscovering" that students who physically write out their
otes by hand have a much greater retention rate than
nose who simply hear or visually read the information.
pparently, God knew this to be true for the kings of
rael also.

rom such understanding came the conception of this series
books.

ave a great time writing and learning the Word of God,

ob Wynalda
omans 1:16

‾he Purpose of the Journible®

‾ngagement:

‾he Journible® is a profoundly simple attempt to aid a
‾erson's ability to engage the Word of God by slowing
‾own the process of simply reading the text. The book is
‾rganized so that the "scribe" can slowly and thoughtfully
‾ngage the text while leaving plenty of room to write
‾omments and questions about the text (Deuteronomy 17:18;
‾salm 119; 2 Timothy 3:16, 17).

‾egacy:

‾ournibles® provide a legacy to pass on from one generation
‾ the next. The Journible® creates an opportunity for one
‾eneration to communicate in writing to the next generation
‾heir insights and personal applications of the text
‾Deuteronomy 6).

‾ow to use this book

‾his book is organized so that the scribe (you) will
‾andwrite your very own copy of Leviticus. You will be
‾riting the text of the Bible only on the right-hand page
‾f the book. This should make for easier writing and also
‾llows ample space on the left page of your open text to
‾rite your own notes and comments. From time to time a
‾uestion or word will be lightly printed on the left page;
‾hese questions are to aid in further study, but should not
‾terfere with your own notes and comments. This means
‾hat you are encouraged not only to write your own "copy"
‾f the Bible, but also to write your own notes concerning
‾he text.

‾es, we are setting aside our mass-produced Gutenberg
‾ibles and attempting to get back to the simple handwritten
‾opy of the text.

Notes

(2) As mediator between God and His people what was Moses's main responsibility?

(3–17) What was the purpose of a burnt offering? See Hebrews 10:1–4.

(3) Why did the bullock have to be "without blemish"? How does this point to Christ (1 Peter 1:19)?

(4) What is the significance of the laying of hands on the sacrifice and how does it relate to the idea of atonement? See 16:21.

(5) What does the death of the bullock teach us about the wages of sin?

Leviticus 1:1-6

Notes

(9) What is symbolically pictured in the burnt offering being a soothing aroma to God (Eph. 5:2)?

(12) What do the altar and sacrifice teach us about the nature of the Christian life? See Romans 12:1–2.

Notes

(13) What is the purpose of the sacrifice being washed with water?

(14) Why would God allow a bird for a burnt offering?

3

4

5

6

7

Notes

(1) What is a grain offering? What is its relation to the other sacrifices, being the only bloodless offering?

(2) What does the costliness and sweet aroma of frankincense teach us about the grain offering?

(4) What is symbolized in the anointing of the grain offering with oil?

(6–7) How do these detailed rituals contrast to the worship commanded in the New Testament? What does this teach us about new covenant worship? See John 4:21–24.

2

3

4

5

6

Notes

(12) What are the "firstfruits"? What is confessed in offering them to the Lord?

7

8

9

10

11

12

Notes

(13) Why was salt necessary? How does this relate to God's covenant relationship with His people? See Numbers 18:19.

13

14

15

16

Notes

(1) What is the purpose of the peace offering?

(2) Why is blood sprinkled upon the altar?

(5) Who eats of this offering? See Deuteronomy 12:7.

2

3

4

5

Notes

(6) What does the word "peace" mean? How does this relate to fellowship with the Lord?

6

7

8

9

10

11

Notes

(16) In ancient Israel the fat was considered the best part of the animal. How does offering this show honor to the Lord? See 1 Samuel 2:15–17, 29.

(17) What did the blood of the sacrifice represent?

12

13

14

15

16

17

Notes

(2) What is an unintentional sin? See Psalm 19:12.

(2–35) What does the need for sacrifice teach us about the seriousness of sin, even when committed inadvertently?

(3) How does the sinfulness of the priests serve to display the unique glory of Christ (Heb. 9:14)?

(6) Why is the blood sprinkled in front of the veil? How does this differ from Christ's priestly ministry (Heb. 6:19–20)?

1

2

3

4

5

6

Notes

Leviticus 4:7-11

7

8

9

10

11

Notes

(12) Why is the bull taken outside the camp? See Hebrews 13:11–13.

(13) What does congregational sin teach us about the corporate nature of God's covenant community?

(15) Why are the elders to lay their hands upon the head of the sacrifice?
What does this reveal about their role and responsibility?

12

13

14

15

16

17

Notes

18

19

20

21

22

23

Notes

(24) Who killed the sacrifice and cut it into sections?
What does this teach us about the self-sacrifice of Christ (Gal. 1:4)?

(28) Where are believers to go when they realize their guilt for unintentional sins?

24

25

26

27

28

Notes

(30) Why is the blood only applied to the horns of the altar? See 4:6, 7, 17, 18, 25.

29

30

31

32

33

Notes

(35) What is the benefit of forgiveness?

(35) How did the sin offering point to Christ in whom alone is found forgiveness? See Hebrews 10:11–14.

34

35

Notes

(1–5) How does failure to do what God requires lead to a guilty conscience?

Leviticus 5:1-5

1

2

3

4

5

Notes

(6) What is atonement? Why does sin necessitate it?

(7) What does God's willingness to accept doves or flour (v. 11) in the place of a lamb teach us about His grace?

6

7

8

9

10

Notes

(15) Is there a difference between the trespass offering (5:15) and the sin offering (4:3)?

11

12

13

14

15

Notes

(16) What does it mean to "make amends"? What does this teach us about sin as debt to God?

(16) How does Christ fulfill the trespass offering in making restitution for our sin? See Isaiah 53:10.

(17) How can a person be guilty but have no knowledge of their sin?

16

17

18

19

Notes

(2) Why are sins committed against men chiefly against God? See Psalm 51:4.

(4) What is the role and function of the conscience in relation to sin?

(4–5) Why does the trespass offering require restitution to one's fellow man when applicable? See Matthew 5:23–26.

Notes

(10–11) What does the priest's removal of the ashes teach us about the sacredness of practical service to God?

(12) How do the daily sacrifices under the old covenant differ from the sacrifice of the new covenant? See Hebrews 7:27.

Notes

(13) Why is it important for the fire to burn upon the alta perpetually? What does this symbolize?

(17) What makes an offering "most holy"?

13

14

15

16

17

18

Notes

(24–27) The priest, tabernacle, and offering are all characterized by holiness. What does "holy" mean?

19

20

21

22

23

24

25

Notes

(28) Why would the earthen vessel in which the offering was boiled be broken?

26

27

28

29

30

Notes

(1) What does the holiness of the offering indicate about how it is to be handled by the priest?

(3) Why are the fat portions to be offered up in fire?

Leviticus 7:1-7

Notes

(11–16) What are the three types of peace offerings and what do they reveal about the heart motivation of the offerer?

8

9

0

1

2

3

Notes

(15) The peace offering was the only offering in which the offerer partook. What is the significance of this picture of feasting with the Lord?

(18) What does "imputed" mean and how does it relate to bearing iniquity?

4

5

6

7

8

Notes

(19–21) What does the divine repulsion to uncleanness teach Israel about God?

(21) What does it mean to be "cut off from his people"?

19

20

21

22

23

24

Notes

(26) Why was eating blood forbidden?

(28–36) How do the priests partaking in the offering point to our fellowship with Christ?

25

26

27

28

29

30

Notes

31

32

33

34

35

36

Notes

(37) How does the offering of Christ relate to each of the offerings summarized here?

(38) Why does Moses stress that these offerings were "commanded" by God?

37

38

Notes

(2) What does the need of a sin offering teach us about the inferiority of the Aaronic priesthood?

(6) Why were the priests washed with water?

(7–9) What does the majesty of Aaron's clothing indicate about the role of the high priest?

Leviticus 8:1-7

1

2

3

4

5

6

7

Notes

(8) What is Urim and Thummim and why would Aaron wear it? See Numbers 27:21; Deuteronomy 33:8; I Samuel 14:41.

(10–12) What is the effect of the tabernacle and Aaron being anointed with oil? How does this relate to Christ (Ps. 45:7) and Christians (1 John 2:20)?

8

9

10

11

12

13

14

Notes

(15) Will Moses continue to offer sacrifices for Israel after the institution of the priesthood?

(17) How many times does this chapter say they did "as the LORD commanded"? What is the significance of this repeated phrase for the ministry of the priesthood?

5

6

7

8

9

0

Notes

(23–24) What was symbolized by the blood being placed on different parts of the body?

21

22

23

24

25

Notes

26

27

28

29

30

Notes

(31–32) What does this meal between God and the priests indicate about their relationship?

(33) Why must ordination to the priesthood take seven days? What does the number seven signify?

(34–36) What does the repetition of the Lord's precept indicate about God's worship?

(35) What does the penalty of death teach us about the seriousness of worshiping God according to His commands?

31

32

33

34

35

36

Notes

(1–4) What is the significance of Aaron beginning his priestly service with so many offerings?

(4) What is the reason given for offering the sacrifices?

(5) How important is the obedience of the priests to God's commands?

(6) What is God's glory? Is its manifestation here related t the revelation of God's glory on Sinai? See Exodus 24:16–1

1

2

3

4

5

6

Notes

(7–21) What is the significance of Moses making atonement for himself prior to making atonement for the people?

7

8

9

10

11

12

Notes

3

4

5

6

7

8

Notes

(22) How does Aaron's blessing of the people relate to Christ's blessing of His disciples after His death? See Luke 24:50.

(24) What does the divine fire consuming the sacrifice reveal?

(24) What is the appropriate response when God manifests His glory? Is such demonstrated here?

19

20

21

22

23

24

Notes

(1) What is "strange fire" and what is its relation to the commandment of God?

(2) What does the death of Nadab and Abihu reveal about God? See Numbers 20:12; 1 Samuel 6:19; Acts 5:1–11.

(3) What does Aaron's silence indicate about the state of his soul?

(1–4) What does this incident teach us about acceptable worship? Who determines how God is to be worshiped?

1

2

3

4

5

Notes

(6) Why couldn't the priests mourn for the deaths of Nadab and Abihu?

(9) Why would wine and strong drink be denied the priests while on duty in the tabernacle?

(10–11) How were the priests to help the people to walk faithfully before the Lord?

6

7

8

9

10

11

Notes

Leviticus 10:12-15

12

13

14

15

Notes

(16–20) Why was Moses upset with Eleazar and Ithamar? What was Aaron's response?

16

17

18

19

20

Notes

(1–47) How do these laws concerning clean and unclean animals relate to the priestly duties laid out in Leviticus 10:10–11?

(1–8) What made a land animal clean or unclean?

Notes

(10) What sea creatures were to be considered detestable?

(13–23) What animals are regulated in this section?

Leviticus 11:8-14

8

9

10

11

12

13

14

Notes

(21) Why is God concerned with Israel's diet?

5

6

7

8

9

0

1

2

3

Notes

(27) What is it about death that leads to uncleanness and defilement?

(29–38) How difficult would it be to remain constantly clean

24

25

26

27

28

29

Notes

30

31

32

33

34

35

Notes

36

37

38

39

40

41

Notes

(43) How could a person become detestable and what would that mean for the person's activity among the community?

(44) How could the people of Israel make themselves holy like God

(44) What is the relationship between the ritual cleanness of the animals and the moral cleanness of God's people?

(45) What is the ultimate reason given for keeping the cleanliness laws? What does 1 Peter 1:13–17 tell us about how this relates to the new covenant?

(46–47) What is the relationship of these cleanliness laws and Israel's separation for the other nations?
See Leviticus 20:24–26.

42

43

44

45

46

Notes

(46–47) Why have these laws been abolished in the new covenant? See Acts 10:9–28.

:47

Notes

(2) What does the ceremonial uncleanness associated with childbirth indicate about the spiritual condition of children? See Psalm 51:5.

(3) What was the purpose of circumcision and how is it related to the depravity into which children are born?

3) What is the spiritual reality to which circumcision points? See Romans 2:29.

(6–7) How did these sacrifices provided for a woman's uncleanness anticipate the Christ to come?

Leviticus 12:1-6

2

3

4

5

6

Notes

(8) What does this indicate about the economic status of Jesus' earthly parents? See Luke 2:22–24.

7

8

Notes

(2–59) What do the meticulous details concerning skin disease indicate about God's desire for cleanliness among His people?

(2) Where is an Israelite to go when he perceives signs of serious skin disease? Why?

(3) How would being declared unclean impact a person's life?

(4–6) Why would God be concerned with the skin of His people?

1

2

3

4

5

Notes

6

7

8

9

10

11

Notes

(15) What spiritual lesson was God teaching Israel through laws about physical uncleanness? See 2 Corinthians 7:1.

2

3

4

5

6

7

8

Notes

(22) Why might disease that spreads be more dangerous than an isolated sore? What might this teach us about sin?

19

20

21

22

23

24

Notes

25

26

27

28

29

Notes

(30) Why might a blemish deeper than the skin be more dangerous? What might this teach us about spiritual defilement?

Leviticus 13:30-34

30

31

32

33

34

Notes

35

36

37

38

39

40

41

Notes

(45) What is communicated by torn clothing, the hair hanging loose, and the covering of the upper lip?

(46) What does the removal of the unclean person from the camp of Israel indicate about God's chosen people?

42

43

44

45

46

47

Notes

(53) What does the priest's role of careful examination and authoritative declaration teach us about the role of elders in the church? See 1 Corinthians 5.

48

49

50

51

52

53

Notes

54

55

56

57

58

Notes

59

Notes

(2) How does the hopelessness of chapter 13 give way to hope here? What does this tell us about God?

(4) Why are cedarwood, scarlet yarn, and hyssop to be used in this cleansing ritual? See Numbers 19:6.

(6) How do the death and life resident in the two birds point forward to Christ?

1

2

3

4

5

6

Notes

(7) What is the symbolism behind the second bird going free? Is it related to the scapegoat of Leviticus 16:6–10?

(10) Why must the healed leper bring two lambs (vv. 12–13)? What does this suggest about how we are cleaned from sin? See 1 John 1:7.

Notes

(14–17) Why are only certain "right" body parts anointed with blood and oil?

2

3

4

5

6

Notes

(21–32) Why does God make concessions to His requirements

7

8

9

0

Notes

22

23

24

25

26

27

Notes

28

29

30

31

32

33

Notes

(34) What does this verse teach us about God's sovereignty in the affliction of His people?

Leviticus 14:34-39

34

35

36

37

38

39

Notes

10

11

12

13

14

Notes

45

46

47

48

49

50

Notes

Leviticus 14:51-57

51

52

53

54

55

56

57

Notes

(2) What spiritual truth is signified in the uncleanness produced by bodily discharges?

(6) How is this uncleanness transferable? What does this teach us about the contaminating power of sin? See 1 Corinthians 15:33

2

3

4

5

6

7

Notes

(11) What was the purpose behind washing and bathing?

8

9

10

11

12

13

Notes

Leviticus 15:14-18

4

5

6

7

8

Notes

(19) Is the woman's uncleanness viewed as a sin?

19

20

21

22

23

24

Notes

(25–30) What is the redemptive significance of Jesus healing one who was ceremonially unclean according to this law? See Matthew 9:20–22.

25

26

27

28

29

Notes

(31) What is the relationship between ceremonial cleanness and God's worship? How does cleansing in Christ relate to new covenant worship?

(32–33) What do all the uncleanness laws of chapter 15 have in common?

30

31

32

33

Notes

(1) What is the connection between the death of Nadab and Abihu and the institution of the day of atonement?

(2) What is the mercy seat and why was Israel restricted in their access to it? How has this changed with Christ? See Matthew 27:51.

(3–4) Why the elaborate preparation to enter the sanctuary? Does God expect the same preparation to approach Him today?

Leviticus 16:1-5

1

2

3

4

5

Notes

(10) How is Christ's one sacrifice pictured in the two goats? Explain how the two goats relate to expiation and propitiation.

6

7

8

9

10

11

Notes

(13) How does the cloud of incense keep the high priest from dying? See Exodus 33:20.

2

3

4

5

6

Notes

(21) What is the significance of Aaron's confession of the sins of the people upon the head of the scapegoat?

17

18

19

20

21

Notes

22

23

24

25

26

Notes

(29) What is indicated by this affliction of soul and how is it related to repentance?

(30) How is this yearly ritual for cleansing from sin fulfilled once-for-all in Christ? See Hebrews 9:23–28.

(31) What is the Sabbath regulation and why would its practice be required on this day? Explain how it was fulfilled in Christ (Col. 2:16–17).

27

28

29

30

31

32

Notes

(34) How are we to understand the "everlasting" nature of this ritual in light of Christ's redemptive work? See Hebrews 13:20.

33

34

Notes

(1–2) Moses functioned as a mediator between Israel and God. Do we still need a mediator today? If yes, who is he?

(3–4) How would this law apply to everyday meals? See Deuteronomy 12:20–23.

1

2

3

4

5

6

Notes

(7) Why is idolatry described as whoredom? What does this indicate about Israel's relationship to God?

(8) Who were resident aliens and what was expected of them?

(9) What is the penalty inflicted on the one who fails to bring the blood of the slain animal to the sanctuary?

(11) What is the reason given for not eating the blood? What does this teach about the death which our sin incurs?

(11) God declares that He is the one who has "given" the blood to His people. What does this teach us about the origin or source of our salvation?

7

8

9

10

11

Notes

12

13

14

15

16

Notes

(1–30) How are the prohibitions of this chapter rooted in creation? What implications does this have for their abiding validity today?

(2–4) Since the Lord is Israel's God, what does He expect from them?

(5) What does this verse teach about the function of the law? See Romans 10:5.

(6–18) What types of sexual relations are forbidden by God here?

2

3

4

5

6

7

Notes

Notes

(19) What is the purpose of this law? How does it relate t
the ceremonial uncleanness spoken of in Leviticus 15:19–24

(21) What does it mean to offer children to Molech?
See 2 Kings 23:10.

5

6

7

8

9

0

1

Notes

(22) Why is the word "abomination" used to refer to homosexual acts?

(24–26) What do God's judgments upon the pagan nations for their sexual immorality teach us today?

(26) Why is God concerned with the natives and aliens that will also live in the land?

2

3

4

5

6

7

Notes

(28) What personification is used in this verse to speak of exile from the land?

(30) How does God's covenant with Israel require them to b other than the world?

Leviticus 18:28-30

28

29

30

Notes

(1–36) Find all Ten Commandments in these verses.

(2) How could Israel obey the command to be holy like God?

Notes

(8) What is the problem with eating three-day old meat? See Leviticus 7:16–18.

(9–10) How do these commands reveal the Lord's character? See Deuteronomy 10:18–19. In what ways could they be carried out by Christians today?

(12) Why is God concerned with the usage of His name?

8

9

10

12

13

Notes

(14) Why does God give specific commands concerning the blind and deaf?

(17–18) What does the place of the heart and the command to love teach about the nature of old covenant religion?

(18) What does it mean to love your neighbor as yourself? How does this summarize the second table of the law? See Matthew 22:39; Romans 13:9.

(19) What is symbolically taught in this law against crossbreeding animals and mixing materials?

14

15

16

17

18

19

Notes

20

21

22

23

24

Notes

(26–30) In what ways were the Israelites called to be different from the surrounding nations here?

25

26

27

28

29

30

31

Notes

(32) What does God's concern for the elderly reveal about Him? See Isaiah 3:5.

(34) What is the reason given for welcoming strangers into the land? See Deuteronomy 10:19.

(35–36) Why is God concerned with honest scales? Apply this today.

32

33

34

35

36

37

Notes

(1) Why is the Lord only speaking through Moses? How does this point to Jesus? See Deuteronomy 18:15.

(2) How does the God-man Jesus Christ differ from the pagan god Molech? See Matthew 19:13–15.

(3) In what ways do people sacrifice their children to false gods today?

(6) What is indicated by the Lord turning His face against someone? See Numbers 6:24–26.

1

2

3

4

5

6

Notes

(8) How is sanctification God's work and also the work of His people? See Philippians 2:12–13.

(10–21) What punishments are commanded for these various sexual sins? What do they indicate about the seriousness of such sin?

7

8

9

10

11

12

Notes

(13) What sin is forbidden here?

13

14

15

16

17

Notes

(22) What is the relationship between Israel's obedience and their remaining in the land?

18

19

20

21

22

Notes

(24) How does Israel's need of holiness relate to the indispensability of holiness in the new covenant? See Hebrews 12:14.

(26) God says of Israel, "Mine." How should this motivate them to holiness and separateness from the world?

3

4

5

6

7

Notes

(1–24) Why was ritual holiness essential for the priests in the fulfillment of their office?

(1) Why did contact with the dead bring about uncleanness? See Numbers 19:11.

(5–6) How did these activities profane God's name? See Leviticus 19:27–28.

Notes

(7) Why was it necessary for the marriage of priests to be marked by holiness?

(8) What does it mean that the Lord was their sanctifier? See Leviticus 21:15, 23; 22:9, 16, 32.

(10–15) Why was the high priest held to stricter standard of ritual holiness than the ordinary priests?

Notes

(17–20) Why would a physical defect affect one's ability enter the sanctuary and make an offering?
How does this point forward to the perfection of Christ?

3

4

5

6

7

8

9

0

Notes

21

22

23

24

Notes

(2) How could the uncleanness of the priest profane the offering?

(3) How is being cut off from the divine presence more severe than being cut off from the people? See Leviticus 19:8; 20:5.

Notes

(9) What is the difference between uncleanness and sinfulness

(10–16) Upon what conditions can lay people eat the offerings of the tabernacle?
Upon what conditions would it lead to death? Why?

7

8

9

10

11

12

Notes

3

4

5

6

7

8

Notes

(19–20) Why must the sacrifice be a perfect male without blemish? How does Christ fulfill this? See Hebrews 7:26; 9:14; 1 Peter 1:19.

(21–25) What did it convey when God's people failed to offer Him such unblemished sacrifices? See Malachi 1:10–14

(23) Why would God allow a freewill offering not to be perfect

9

20

1

2

3

4

Notes

(30) What does the need to consume a thanksgiving offering on the same day indicate about its importance? See Leviticus 7:15–16.

25

26

27

28

29

30

31

Notes

(32) What does it mean for the Lord not only to sanctify His people, but to be sanctified among them?

(33) Why does God remind them of their redemption from Egypt?

32

33

Notes

(2) What is a holy convocation? How would such a sacred assembly foster fellowship with God and with God's people?

(3) What does the word "Sabbath" mean?
What was God's purpose in giving man the Sabbath?

(3) How was the Sabbath foundational to the other feasts of Israel?

(5–22) What were the three spring feasts?

(5–8) How does Christ fulfill the Passover Feast?
See Luke 22:7–20; 1 Corinthians 5:7.

2

3

4

5

Notes

(9–14) What was celebrated at the Feast of Firstfruits? Why were the firstfruits of the harvest offered to the Lord?

8

9

10

11

12

13

Notes

(15–22) What is another name for the Feast of Weeks? What significant event took place on this day in the book of Acts?

14

15

16

17

18

Notes

(22) Why did God command that crops be left in the fields?

(23–36) What were the three fall feasts?

(23–25) As the first day of the seventh month, what did the Feast of Trumpets mark in the Hebrew calendar?

19

20

21

22

23

24

Notes

(27) What did it mean for the Israelites to "afflict" their souls on the Day of Atonement?

(28–32) Why does God here focus on the people's acts rather than the ceremonial rituals of this day?

25

26

27

28

29

30

31

Notes

(33–36) What was the purpose of the Feast of Booths? What was it to remind the Israelites of (vv. 39–43)?

32

33

34

35

36

37

Notes

Leviticus 23:38-42

38

39

40

41

42

Notes

43

44

Notes

(1) Why does the Lord place this command concerning the ordinary, daily work of the tabernacle just after the description of the feast calendar?

(2) Where was the lamp and why must it always be lit? See Exodus 25:31–39; 27:20–21.

(4) How do the candlesticks represent Christ (Luke 2:32) and His churches (Rev. 1:13)?

(5) What did the twelve loaves dwelling in God's presence symbolize?

1

2

3

4

5

6

7

Notes

(9) When David ate this bread why wasn't he punished? See Matthew 12:1–8.

(12) Why did the people wait for specific revelation from God concerning the necessary penalty for this man's blasphemy?

8

9

10

11

12

13

Notes

(14) Why did God demand the laying on of hands prior to stoning?

(16) Rather than saying he blasphemed God, Moses says he blasphemed "the Name"? What does this indicate about the relationship of God's name to Himself?

(19–20) What is the general principle of this command? How does Jesus' teaching in Matthew 5:38–39 relate to this?

14

15

16

17

18

19

20

Notes

21

22

23

Notes

(1–22) How does the weekly Sabbath relate to the Sabbath Year and the Jubilee Year?

(2) What was the purpose of the Sabbath rest for the land?

(5–7) What did God expect them to eat during the Sabbath Year? How did this teach them to look to God for their needs?

1

2

3

4

5

6

7

Notes

(9) Why was the Day of Atonement significant to the year of Jubilee? See Luke 4:18–19.

(10) Why would God command Israel to celebrate this year of release and liberty?

Leviticus 25:8-13

Notes

(17) What does it mean to fear God? What is the relationshi
between fearing God and loving our neighbor?

(18–22) What were the blessings that obedience to the Sabbath Year and Jubilee Year brought about?

4

5

6

7

8

9

0

Notes

(23) In what sense would the Israelites function as sojourners in the land of promise? For whom were they to steward the land

(25) How was the kinsman-redeemer a foreshadowing of Jesus Christ?

(26–28) What was the right of redemption? Why was land not to be permanently sold from one family to another

21

22

23

24

25

26

Notes

27

28

29

30

31

Notes

Leviticus 25:32-37

32

33

34

35

36

37

Notes

(39–40) What is the difference between a slave and an employee?

38

39

40

41

42

43

44

Notes

(45–46) Why does God allow slavery here?

45

46

47

48

49

Notes

(55) Israel was delivered from Egyptian servitude in order to serve the Lord. How is this true of Christians today?

50

51

52

53

54

55

Notes

(1) Why would Israel be tempted to worship stone idols?

(3–13) What are the covenant blessings that God here promises to those who keep covenant with Him?

1

2

3

4

5

6

Notes

(9) What does it mean for God to "confirm" His covenant?

(11–12) What is the significance of the Lord's presence in the midst of His people? How are all covenant blessings summed up in this one?

7

8

9

10

11

12

13

14

Notes

(15) When Israel breaks God's rules, are they breaking the covenant? See Deuteronomy 28.

(15) What does this abhorrence of soul towards God's commands reveal about their heart attitude toward God Himself?

(19) What is pride and why would Israel struggle with it?

(20–26) How do these curses reveal the exhaustive sovereignty of God?

Leviticus 26:15-20

15

16

17

18

19

20

Notes

21

22

23

24

25

26

Notes

(27–39) Why was exile the ultimate curse God would bring upon His people? What did the loss of land signify?

27

28

29

30

31

32

33

Notes

34

35

36

37

38

Notes

(39–42) What are the marks of true repentance set forth here?

(41) What is an uncircumcised heart and why is it important?

42) In what way can God be said to remember?
What does this tell us about His character?

39

40

41

42

43

Notes

(44) What does this verse teach us about God's faithfulness and the immutability of His promise?

44

45

46

Notes

(1) What is the reason behind concluding Leviticus with laws concerning vows and dedication? How do they relate to the funding of the tabernacle?

(2) What are vows understood to be here?

(2–8) What is the purpose of these valuations?

Leviticus 27:1-6

1

2

3

4

5

6

Notes

(8) Why would God make exceptions for a poor man?

(10) What happens if one substitutes one's vowed item? What does this teach us concerning making vows to the Lord?

7

8

9

0

1

2

Notes

(17–24) Why would the Jubilee affect property values?

13

14

15

16

17

18

Notes

19

20

21

22

23

24

Notes

(25) How much buying power was in a shekel?

(26) Why can't the firstborn be vowed?

(30–33) What is a tithe? Are we to practice tithing today? See Genesis 28:20–22; Matthew 23:23.

25

26

27

28

29

30

Notes

(34) What is the significance of Israel receiving the entire book of Leviticus from Mount Sinai?

How would these laws have encouraged them in their journey toward the promised land?

31

32

33

34

Notes

Notes

Notes

Notes

Notes